This book belongs to

....

It was given to me by

....

Date

....

Jesus
Loves
Me

Sketchbook
& Journal

Published by CR3ATIVE Group (3CG), Grandville, Michigan.

Printed in the United States of America.

Welcome

to the *Jesus Loves Me Sketchbook & Journal.*

We're glad you're here! This book is a place for you to learn more about two very important people—Jesus and me. And by "me," we mean *you*!

Maybe you've sung the song "Jesus Loves Me." Maybe your great-great-grandparents did—did you know that song was written more than 150 years ago? But its message never changes, because Jesus never changes. He loves you, and wants you to be part of His family forever.

So in this journal, you'll learn some great things about Jesus, who is the Son of God. At the same time, He *is* God. We know—that's hard to understand, but it's true. God the Father, Jesus the Son, and the Holy Spirit are one Person we call "the Trinity."

The Trinity loves you, and everything about you. God made you, and He gave you all the skills and interests and qualities that make you so special. The *Jesus Loves Me Sketchbook & Journal* is a way to thank Him for making you *you*.

Whether you like to write or draw or color (or all three), this book is for you. We hope you enjoy it. . .and we especially hope you'll get to know Jesus better. (Did we mention that He loves you?)

The Editors

"For this is how God loved the world: He gave his one and only Son, so that everyone who believes in him will not perish but have eternal life."

John 3:16 NLT

Section 1

Jesus Loves Me–This I Know

Love is patient and kind.

1 Corinthians 13:4 ncv

Jesus loves me

just as much when I'm ....
as when I'm ....

*(Fill in the blanks with words from the list below. Then draw
a picture that reminds you of Jesus' amazing love.)*

funny	bad	good
sad	angry	happy

(or pick your own words!)

Write, Draw, Color, Create!

Jesus loves me. . .

- [ ] as high as the sky

- [ ] to the bottom of the deepest ocean

- [ ] far into outer space

- [ ] to the tops of the tallest trees
  in the forest

- [ ] more than anything I could
  ever imagine

Write, Draw, Color, Create!

When I think about how
much Jesus loves me, I. . .

- ☐ smile
- ☐ feel all warm and fuzzy
- ☐ think of how much I
  love Him back
- ☐ want to share His love
  with all my friends

When I think of Jesus' love, my face looks like this:

(Draw yourself in the space below!)

One word that reminds me of how much Jesus loves me is _____.

(Write the special word you've chosen in bubble letters. . .and fill it in with your favorite colors!)

Write, Draw, Color, Create!

I don't ever need to feel sad
or lonely because Jesus. . .

- [ ] is always here for me
- [ ] hears my prayers
- [ ] understands exactly how I feel
- [ ] knows my name
- [ ] is my very best Friend

Write, Draw, Color, Create!

Jesus cares about people, including:

- ☐ ME!
- ☐ my BFFs
- ☐ bullies
- ☐ my family
- ☐ my teacher
- ☐ my neighbors
- ☐ EVERYONE!

Here's a picture of
me and my BFFs:

RANDOM HAPPY DOODLES!

Things that make me happy:

1.
2.
3.
4.
5.
6. Jesus' love!

Write, Draw, Color, Create!

I have many
blessings in my life.
Just to name a few. . .

1. ....

2. ....

3. ....

4. ....

5. ....

6. Jesus' love!

Write, Draw, Color, Create!

Write, Draw, Color, Create!

When I think about how
Jesus has blessed me, I feel

- ☐ happy!
- ☐ like singing
- ☐ like dancing
- ☐ like hugging someone
- ☐ like telling everyone
  how good He is!
- ☐ all of the above

Because of Jesus' amazing love,
I can plant seeds of joy wherever I go.

Here is a picture of me planting a seed of joy!

Write, Draw, Color, Create!

Jesus is with me. . .

☐ when I pray

☐ when I play

☐ when I sleep

☐ when I eat

☐ anywhere

☐ everywhere

☐ always!

And because He is with me, I never
need to feel lonely or afraid!

If I had a conversation with Jesus, I think we'd talk about:

If Jesus came to my house for a visit, here's what we'd do:

And now, my children,
live by the help of Him.
Then when He comes again,
we will be glad to see Him
and not be ashamed.
1 JOHN 2:28 NLV

Because of Jesus and His love for me,
I can *always* do the right thing.

Here is a picture of me doing the right thing:

The Bible says that a
cheerful heart is good medicine.

Here is a picture of me with a cheerful heart!

A glad heart is
good medicine.
PROVERBS 17:22 NLV

RANDOM HAPPY DOODLES!

Things that make my heart glad:

1. ....
2. ....
3. ....
4. ....
5. Jesus!

Write, Draw, Color, Create!

Family is important to
God—after all, He chose
mine just for me.

Here are some fun facts about my family:

1. ....

2. ....

3. ....

4. ....

5. ....

Write, Draw, Color, Create!

Here's a picture of my family—and me!

"But as for me and
my family, we will
serve the Lord."
JOSHUA 24:15 NLV

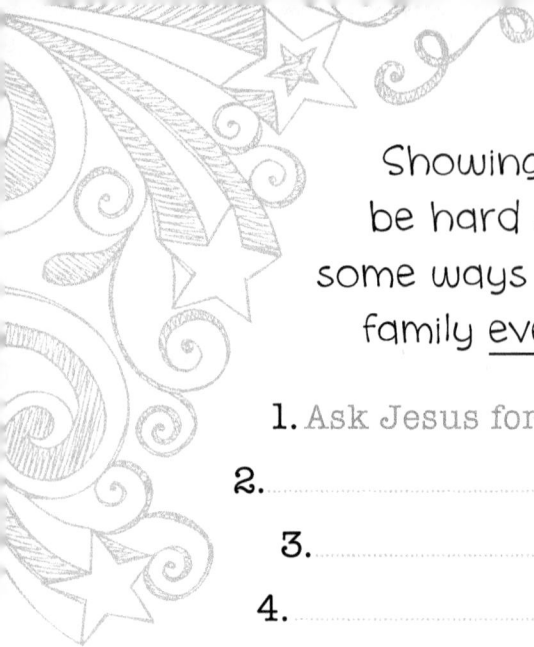

Showing love to others can
be hard sometimes. Here are
some ways I can show love to my
family every day of the week.

1. Ask Jesus for help, and. . .

2.

3.

4.

5.

Write, Draw, Color, Create!

Write, Draw, Color, Create!

God always wants to
hear my prayers.

Here are some things I'm praying about this week:

1. ....

2. ....

3. ....

4. ....

5. ....

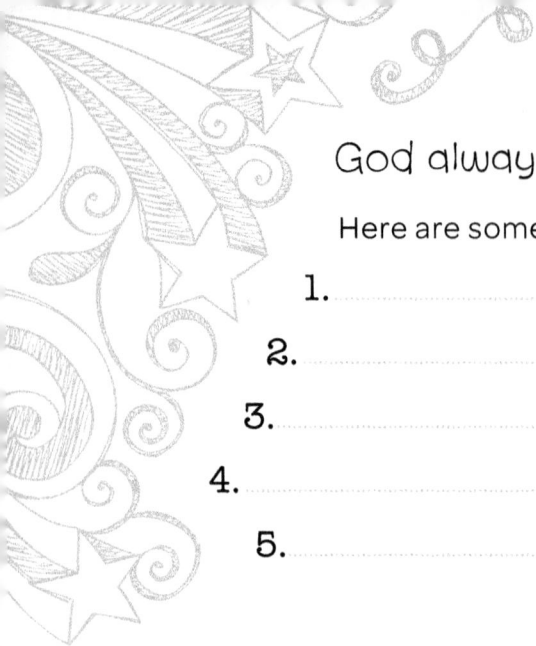

God always listens to my prayers.

Here are some prayers He's answered for me:

1. ....
2. ....
3. ....
4. ....
5. ....

Write, Draw, Color, Create!

Section 2

. . .for the Bible Tells Me So

Think how much the Father loves us.
He loves us so much that he
lets us be called his children,
as we truly are.

1 JOHN 3:1 CEV

Write, Draw, Color, Create!

I know Jesus loves me because. . .

- ☐ He made me
- ☐ He forgives me
- ☐ He listens to me
- ☐ He protects me
- ☐ He understands me
- ☐ He offers me eternal life
- ☐ He keeps His promises
- ☐ the Bible tells me so!
- ☐ all of the above

Jesus' love makes me happy!

Draw a picture in your favorite "happy color"!

Write, Draw, Color, Create!

Because Jesus loves me,
He made me. . .

- ☐ unique
- ☐ strong
- ☐ smart
- ☐ talented
- ☐ kind
- ☐ caring
- ☐ funny
- ☐ ....
  (fill in the blank!)

I am so thankful for the Bible because

....

(Draw a picture of you reading your
Bible in your favorite place.)

Write, Draw, Color, Create!

God made me special and unique.

My favorite thing about *me* is:

☐ the color of my eyes

☐ the color of my hair

☐ my nose

☐ my chin

☐ my toes

☐ ....
(fill in the blank!)

Here is a picture of my
<u>favorite</u> thing about ME!

RANDOM HAPPY DOODLES!

Can anything make Jesus love me more?

☐ Yes

☐ No

Can anything make Jesus love me less?

☐ Yes

☐ No

Jesus ALWAYS loves me—
NO MATTER WHAT!

"This is my command: Love each other
as I have loved you. The greatest love a person
can show is to die for his friends."
JOHN 15:12-13 NCV

I am thankful for my favorites. . .

My favorite color

My favorite animal

My favorite holiday

My favorite food

My favorite place

My favorite teacher

My favorite friend

My favorite book

My favorite movie

Write, Draw, Color, Create!

The Bible gives answers for
__EVERYTHING!__ including. . .

☐ how this great big beautiful world came to be

☐ how to treat other people

☐ what to do when I'm afraid

☐ how to pray

☐ ....

And best of all, the Bible never
changes—NOT EVER!

The grass withers and the flowers fade,
but the word of our God stands forever.
ISAIAH 40:8 NLT

Jesus was always giving to
the people around Him. And
He wants me to do the same!

Here are some ideas for sharing my stuff with
those who are in need. . .

1.

2.

3.

4.

5.

God always does what is right. He will not
forget the work you did to help the Christians
and the work you are still doing to help
them. This shows your love for Christ.
HEBREWS 6:10 NLV

Write, Draw, Color, Create!

Write, Draw, Color, Create!

Some people say I'm too young to make
an impact on the world around me.

But, with help from Jesus, here are some ways I can do good for
others in my school, the community, even in my own house:

1.

2.

3.

4.

5.

> *Whatever work you do, do it with all your heart.*
> *Do it for the Lord and not for men. Remember*
> *that you will get your reward from the Lord.*
> *He will give you what you should receive.*
> *You are working for the Lord Christ.*
> COLOSSIANS 3:23–24 NLV

Some things I struggle with:

- ☐ homework
- ☐ chores
- ☐ bullies
- ☐ teachers who just don't "get me"
- ☐ having patience with my family
- ☐ all of the above

But the good news is that Jesus can help me to honor Him in all of these areas. All I have to do is ask!

God has given me His Word to help me make good choices in life. Things like—

Healthy snack? . . . Or junk food?

Fighting back? . . . Or walking away?

Finishing that school project? . . .
Or playing a video game instead?

Saving my birthday money? . . .
Or blowing my birthday money on a
toy I won't care about in a week?

Sticking up for someone who's being bullied? . . .
Or pretending not to notice the bullying?

What's your choice? . . .
Circle the choices you would make in each situation.

Do as God would do. Much-loved
children want to do as their fathers do.
EPHESIANS 5:1 NLV

Here is a picture of me
making a good choice.

Jesus loves me so much. He always knows exactly what's going on in my heart.

This is what's going on in my heart today.
(Draw a picture in the space below.)

Things that make me feel afraid:

☐ spiders

☐ the dark

☐ bullies

☐ thunderstorms

☐ ....
(write your biggest fear here)

But because of Jesus and His amazing love for me,
I don't ever have to be afraid of anything!

Write, Draw, Color, Create!

Write, Draw, Color, Create!

Things that make me feel brave:

- ☐ my best friend
- ☐ my favorite stuffed animal
- ☐ talking to Jesus
- ☐ reading the Bible
- ☐ ....
  (fill in the blank!)

I think Jesus cares
about small things like:

1. ....

2. ....

3. ....

4. ....

5. ....

Write, Draw, Color, Create!

Write, Draw, Color, Create!

. . .and I think Jesus cares
about BIG things like:

1.
2.
3.
4.
5.

RANDOM HAPPY DOODLES!

Today, if I could change just one thing about the world,
it would be:

I am so thankful for my
favorite people, including:

1. ....

2. ....

3. ....

4. ....

5. ....

Write, Draw, Color, Create!

Here is a picture of my favorite person!

Draw a picture of something that
always makes you laugh.

Jesus has placed many dreams in my heart.

One of those dreams is. . .

(Draw or write about your dream in the space below.)

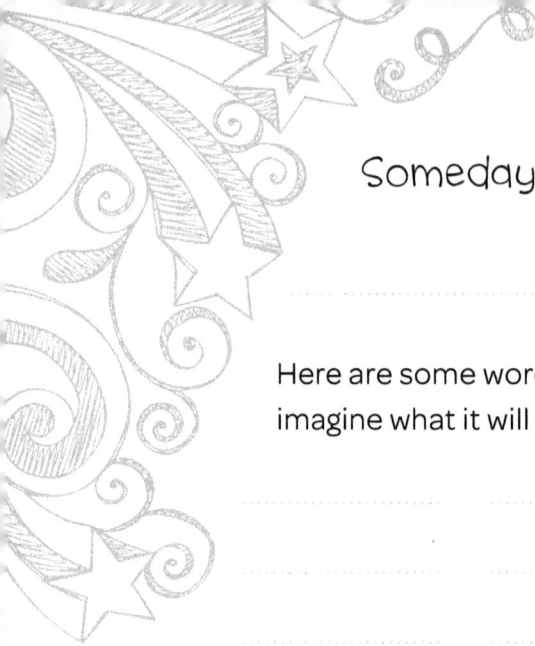

Someday, I hope to visit

....

Here are some words that come to mind when I
imagine what it will be like:

....

....

....

Write, Draw, Color, Create!

Write, Draw, Color, Create!

Jesus is <u>always</u> happy
to hear from me.

Here are some things I need to talk to Him
about this week:

My favorite place to talk to Jesus is

....

(Draw a picture of You talking to God in the space below.)

Today, I'm feeling ....

(Draw a picture that shows how you feel today.)

Write, Draw, Color, Create!

Having Jesus as my friend
makes me feel. . .

- ☐ so very happy
- ☐ energetic
- ☐ like being kind to others
- ☐ like singing a song
- ☐ like whistling a tune
- ☐ like jumping for joy!
- ☐ all of the above

Section 3

Little Ones to Him Belong

*"For I know the plans I have for you,"
declares the Lord, "plans to prosper
you and not to harm you, plans to
give you hope and a future."*
JEREMIAH 29:11 NIV

When I grow up,
I want to be a

.... ,

because ....

Write, Draw, Color, Create!

Here is a picture of the grown-up me!

RANDOM HAPPY DOODLES!

God gave me many talents.

- ☐ I am a great singer
- ☐ I love to dance
- ☐ I am an artist in the making
- ☐ I am good at sports
- ☐ ....
  (fill in the blank with another special talent!)

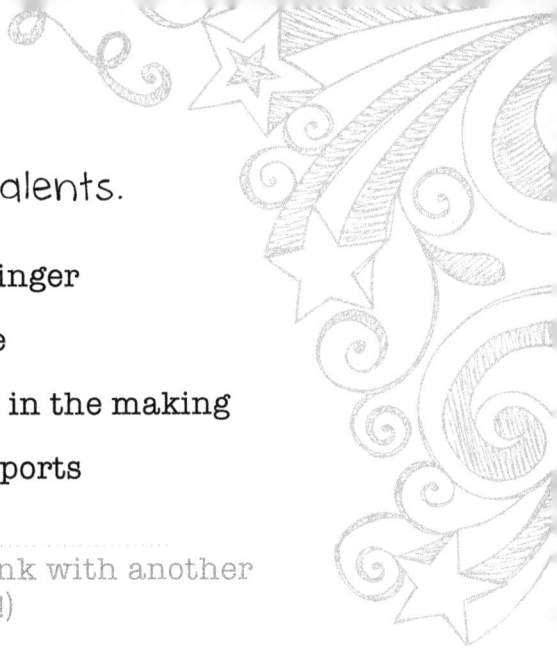

Write, Draw, Color, Create!

Here is what I hope for the most:

....

Write, Draw, Color, Create!

When bad things happen, I can:

- ☐ talk to Jesus
- ☐ talk to a good friend
- ☐ share my feelings with Mom or Dad
- ☐ read the Bible
- ☐ ....
  (fill in the blank)

Uh-oh! Here is my "worried" face:

Here is my "I just talked to Jesus and everything's going to be okay" face:

Jesus knows me better than. . .

- [ ] Mom
- [ ] Dad
- [ ] Grandma and Grandpa
- [ ] my BFF
- [ ] me
- [ ] anyone else in the whole entire universe!

Write, Draw, Color, Create!

Write, Draw, Color, Create!

Jesus gives me:

- ☐ happiness
- ☐ love
- ☐ hope
- ☐ friends and family
- ☐ everything I need!

Jesus cares most about my:

- ☐ clothes
- ☐ neatness
- ☐ grades
- ☐ cool new shoes
- ☐ amazing talents
- ☐ HEART!

"The LORD does not look at the things
people look at. People look at the outward
appearance, but the Lord looks at the heart."
1 SAMUEL 16:7 NIV

Write, Draw, Color, Create!

Jesus loves me so much, He will
always give me just what I need.

He doesn't always give me everything
I *want*—but sometimes He will!

Make a list of your needs and wants in the space below.

My Needs

....

....

....

My Wants

....

....

....

God. . .will supply all your needs from his glorious
riches, which have been given to us in Christ Jesus.
PHILIPPIANS 4:19 NLT

Write, Draw, Color, Create!

Because I believe in my heart that Jesus died for my sins, I will spend FOREVER in heaven.

I think heaven will be. . .

- [ ] the most awesome place I've ever seen.
- [ ] full of peace and love.
- [ ] PERFECT!
- [ ] like going to the beach, only WAY better.
- [ ] overflowing with God's love.
- [ ] like a warm hug.
- [ ] ....
(fill in the blank!)

Even though I've never seen Jesus,
I sometimes imagine what He looks like.

In my mind, Jesus looks like this:

RANDOM HAPPY DOODLES!

If we belong to Jesus, we should learn to be kind just like Him.

This includes being kind to:

☐ mean girls

☐ my brothers or sisters

☐ my mom and dad

☐ the grumpy neighbor

☐ my pets

☐ ....
(fill in the blank)

Write, Draw, Color, Create!

Today I will be kind to ....

(Draw a picture of you being kind in the space below.)

Because I belong to Jesus,
I can learn to give happily.

Here is what a happy, generous heart looks like.

Draw a picture in the space below.

"God loves a person
who gives cheerfully."
2 CORINTHIANS 9:7 NLT

Roses are red,
Violets are blue,
Because Jesus loves me,

. . . .

. . . .

(Finish the rhyme with your own words.)

Write, Draw, Color, Create!

Write, Draw, Color, Create!

Jesus promises to be my Friend forever!

In the spaces below, write some words that remind you of friendship:

....

....

....

Adjectives are words that describe a person, place, or thing.

In the spaces below, write some adjectives that describe Jesus:

loving

Write, Draw, Color, Create!

When I asked Jesus into my life, He changed my heart. "My heart" is who I really am—my thoughts and emotions and fears and dreams.

My heart used to look like this:

Now it looks like this!

"Though your sins are like scarlet, I will make them as white as snow. Though they are red like crimson, I will make them as white as wool."
ISAIAH 1:18 NLT

Some days are hard. But with
Jesus' help, we can always find joy.
When we spend time with Him,
He can help make things right again.

Here is a picture of me after Jesus makes my hard days better:

Write, Draw, Color, Create!

Jesus' love reminds me of. . .

- [ ] bright sunshine after a storm
- [ ] a warm hug from a friend
- [ ] snuggling with my favorite stuffed animal
- [ ] curling up with a good book
- [ ] ....

I can always count on God's promises.

Draw and color a rainbow in the space below,
as a reminder of His amazing love:

"I have set my rainbow in
the clouds, and it will be the
sign of the covenant between
me and the earth."
GENESIS 9:13 NIV

The Bible tells us to put on "armor" so
we can stand strong against the devil.
Fill in the blanks below. If you need help,
check out Ephesians 6:10–17 NLT.

"Stand your ground, putting on the belt of ....

(verse 14)

and the body armor of God's righteousness. For shoes,

put on the .... that comes from the Good

(verse 15)

News so that you will be fully prepared. In addition to

all of these, hold up the shield of .... to stop

(verse 16)

the fiery arrows of the devil. Put on .... as your

(verse 17)

helmet, and take the sword of the Spirit, which is the

.... "

(verse 17)

Be strong in the Lord and in his mighty power.
Put on all of God's armor so that you will be able
to stand firm against all strategies of the devil.
EPHESIANS 6:10–11 NLT

Here is a picture of me,
wearing the armor of God!

Section 4

. . .They Are Weak
but He Is Strong

*He will cover you with his
feathers, and under his wings
you can hide. His truth will be
your shield and protection.*

PSALM 91:4 NCV

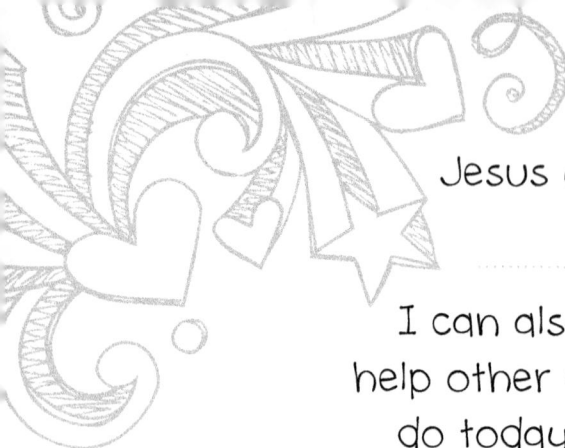

Jesus gives me the strength to

....

I can also use Jesus' strength to
help other people. Something I can
do today to help someone else is

....

Write, Draw, Color, Create!

Here is a picture of me helping a friend:

RANDOM HAPPY DOODLES!

With Jesus' help, I can do
A-M-A-Z-I-N-G things!

Color in the letters. Use your favorite colors!

AMAZING

For we are God's handiwork, created in
Christ Jesus to do good works, which God
prepared in advance for us to do.
EPHESIANS 2:10 NIV

Here is a picture of me doing
something amazing for Jesus:

When I'm afraid, I can think of Jesus and His promises and feel brave again. Here is a Bible verse that gives me courage:

Here is a picture of the BRAVE me:

Write, Draw, Color, Create!

Things that bring me
comfort when I'm scared. . .

- ☐ my favorite stuffed animal
- ☐ my favorite book
- ☐ talking to God
- ☐ reading my Bible
- ☐ a hug from a friend
- ☐ ....
  (fill in the blank!)

Things I worry about. . .

But I *never* have to worry about anything—
because the One who loves me most says so:

When you lie down, you will not be afraid;
when you lie down, your sleep will be sweet.
PROVERBS 3:24 NIV

Write, Draw, Color, Create!

Write, Draw, Color, Create!

I am so glad God created
the world and everything
in it—including ME!

I think He created the world because. . .

- [ ] He is super creative.

- [ ] He wanted me—and everyone
  else—to have a cool place to live.

- [ ] He wants to be my Friend forever.

- [ ] He wants us to be a part of
  His family.

- [ ] He *is* love!

Jesus' love for me is even BIGGER than. . .

(Draw a picture in the space below.)

If I could thank Jesus for just
ONE thing today, it would be this:

Unscramble the words below
for a special message:

SUJES   VELSO   EM!

....!

(Yes, He does!)

y-young

o-outstanding

U-unique

Thank God for creating you just as you are!
(He wouldn't want you any other way!)

Write, Draw, Color, Create!

How many times does Jesus think about you in a day?

- ☐ 1
- ☐ 50
- ☐ 100
- ☐ 1000
- ☐ 1 Million
- ☐ There isn't a number big enough!

RANDOM HAPPY DOODLES!

No matter what, always remember
one very super-duper important thing:

JESUS LOVES YOU.

And that will never ever <u>EVER</u> change!

Design and color the letters below:

LOVE

Write, Draw, Color, Create!

Jesus can give me the strength
to help others be strong.

I can encourage others through my. . .

- [ ] words
- [ ] actions
- [ ] prayers
- [ ] all of the above!

Here is a list of some
super-encouraging words
I can speak to others:

....

....

....

Write, Draw, Color, Create!

Write, Draw, Color, Create!

Jesus will ALWAYS give me the
strength and courage I need to:

☐ stand up to the school bully

☐ study for a really hard test

☐ finish a project I started

☐ share His love with others

☐ ....
(fill in the blank!)

Prayer—the perfect beginning
and ending to your day.

My morning prayer to Jesus is this:

....
....
....
....
....

My nighttime prayer to Jesus is this:

....
....
....
....
....
....

Send up a word of thanks to
Jesus today. . .because the SUNSHINE
will always follow the RAIN.

Draw a picture of the sunshine after a rain shower:

Best 5 Things about Today:

....

....

....

....

....

Send up a great big THANKS to Jesus for these things!

Write, Draw, Color, Create!

Write, Draw, Color, Create!

5 Things I Wish I Could
Change about Today:

....

....

....

....

....

Ask Jesus for a fresh start tomorrow. . . .
He can make ANYTHING better!

Write, Draw, Color, Create!

Because of Jesus, I WILL:

- ☐ choose joy
- ☐ not be afraid
- ☐ dream big!
- ☐ be thankful for the little things
- ☐ be thankful for the big things
- ☐ think before I speak
- ☐ be kind
- ☐ pray!
- ☐ ....
  (fill in the blank!)

Jesus loved me yesterday!

Draw "Baby You" in the space below.

Jesus loves me today!

Draw "Today You" in the space below.

And Jesus will love me tomorrow!

Draw "Future You" in the space below.

Before I was even born,
Jesus had plans for me!

Jesus isn't surprised that. . .

I'm good at ....

I know the most about ....

I laugh loudest when ....

I love to ....

I can do all things because
Christ gives me the strength.
PHILIPPIANS 4:13 NLV

RANDOM HAPPY DOODLES!

Some questions I'd like to ask Jesus:

Why ....

.... ?

How ....

.... ?

What ....

.... ?

Where ....

.... ?

When ....

.... ?

Jesus loves. . .

.... people

.... people

.... people

.... people

.... people

.... people

.... people

.... people

.... people

Fill in the blanks above with words from the list below:

Funny	Silly	Pretty
All	Tall	Lonely
Smart	Talkative	Young
Good	Bossy	Sick
Sad	Strange	Mean
Short	Thin	Happy
Talented	Quiet	Old
Kind	Loud	Healthy

Draw a picture showing the
many types of people Jesus loves:

Jesus loves everyone in the <u>whole entire big</u> world.

Draw a picture of the world in the space below. Then put hearts around it to stand for Jesus' love that goes on forever and ever!

www.ingramcontent.com/pod-product-compliance
Lightning Source LLC
Chambersburg PA
CBHW071559040426
42452CB00008B/1224

9 780979 391156